C000091867

Dicewr

FOR EROTICA & EROTIC ROMANCE

THOUSANDS OF STORY PROMPTS
AND INSPIRATIONS

Zak Jane Keir

Part of the Self-Publishing Shortcuts Series

For books, workshops, online courses and tools to help you generate ideas, write stronger narratives and publish your work more quickly, visit:

www.selfpublishingshortcuts.com

Book Layout © 2018 MyAuthorlyFormatting.com

ISBN 978-1-9807-3975-3

ACKNOWLEDGEMENTS

This book grew out of a workshop session I put together for Smut Leeds in August 2017 and is therefore dedicated with love and thanks to Janine Ashbless, Jennifer Denys, Victoria Blisse and Anna Sky, who all thought that a whole book of charts was a good idea...

CONTENTS

INTRODUCTION

Dicewriting is, first and foremost, a fun way of getting your imagination moving. Beginner or experienced veteran, every author has times of not knowing what to do next, or wanting to write a story for a particular submissions call, but not knowing where to start. Giving yourself a set of random options (the story features an older man with an intimate piercing, it's set up a mountain, and a major plot point involves a cucumber) can send your writing brain off on a variety of journeys, some of which will suit you better than others. If you've been stuck for a long time, it might be the case that a completely absurd juxtaposition of character, prop and ambient climate will get you back in your creative zone: what could you do with a masked stranger, a balmy spring evening and a lost buttplug?

The charts in this book give you thousands of options for stories of any length you like. Most charts will give you a selection of prompts you can use to create a story that's as romantic – or as dark, or as dirty – as you want. Some concepts are extremely open, some are a little more specific, but the interpretation of the terms is mainly up to you – unless the outcome of one dice roll influences the next in a particular direction.

You will need a single, six-sided die. If you don't have one handy, you can use a deck of playing cards (remove the joker) or, if you prefer (and have a deck that means a lot to you), tarot cards.

If you're using playing cards, the values are as follows.

- Ace = 1
- Court card (king, queen, jack) = 2
- Hearts = 3
- Clubs = 4
- Diamonds = 5
- Spades = 6

For tarot cards:

- Major arcana = 1
- King, queen, knight etc = 2
- Wands = 3
- Cups = 4
- Swords = 5
- Coins = 6

WRITERS' GROUPS

If you belong to a group, you can easily hold a dicewriting session at some of your meetings. The Story Starters section is designed with an eye to doing this, and additional options are given so you can make up an extra chart of your own.

CHARACTER CREATION

Often the quickest way into a story is to create a protagonist, or central character. Sometimes, getting your first character inspires you to create someone for this protagonist to lust after – or compete with – and the story simply takes off on its own. Sometimes it's fun to generate two or three characters with dice rolls and think about what would happen if you put these people together.

A PROTAGONIST FOR
ANY EROTICA/EROTIC ROMANCE
STORY

FIRST ROLL

This one is optional, as you may already know that you want to write romantic M/F erotica, MM or FF, or a story containing only genderqueer or non-binary characters.

1) *Lesbian*
2) *Gay*
3) *Bisexual*
4) *Trans*
5) *Queer*
6) *Straight*

You can either roll again to see which of the next six charts you will roll from, or just pick one.

PHYSICAL ASPECTS OR THINGS YOU NOTICE FIRST

V1

1) Short-sighted
2) Young (18-24)
3) Has beautiful hands
4) Is very fidgety
5) Has a distinctive way of dressing
6) Long-haired

V2

1) Very thin
2) Heavily tattooed
3) Clumsy and uncoordinated
4) Bald
5) Long fingernails
6) Is petite

V3
1) Has a facial scar
2) Is big and/or physically imposing
3) Wears glasses
4) Has a distinctive hairstyle
5) Moves gracefully
6) Is over 40

V4
1) Has a striking resemblance to a celebrity
2) Is hearing-impaired
3) Has a facial piercing
4) Dresses very smartly
5) Intimidating/off-putting body language
6) Has dyed hair

V5

1) Has a big bottom
2) Heavily freckled
3) Is wearing a uniform
4) Has a sexy voice
5) Tires easily/has limited strength
6) Has good cheekbones

V6

1) Is elegant
2) Short and chubby
3) Has a lot of body hair
4) Smells delicious
5) Athletic/toned
6) Has good skin

STATE OF MIND OR DISTINCTIVE PERSONALITY TRAIT

M1
1) Is easily led
2) Tends to sulk
3) Has traditional values
4) Is inquisitive
5) Is confident
6) Is suspicious

M2
1) Is grumpy
2) Has a positive outlook
3) Is mischievous
4) Is sensible
5) Is sad
6) Is ashamed of something

M3

1) Pays attention to details
2) Is timid
3) Burning with resentment
4) Is charming
5) Loves music
6) Practices self-denial

M4

1) Is shy
2) Is heartbroken
3) Is ambitious
4) Is very generous
5) Can be over-protective
6) Has strong political convictions

M5
1) Is a daydreamer
2) Is possessive
3) Is usually cheerful
4) Prickly and easily offended
5) Serious-minded
6) Sports-mad

M6
1) Is sensitive
2) Is restless
3) Highly impulsive
4) Romantic
5) Practical and good at fixing things
6) Well-read

P1: THE MOST IMPORTANT THING ABOUT THIS CHARACTER IS

1) The secret they are keeping
2) The intensity of their feelings
3) A criminal past
4) Their lack of experience
5) That they are being blackmailed
6) They are undercover

P2: SOMETHING THEY CARE ABOUT A GREAT DEAL

1) Fidelity/monogamy
2) Their kink
3) Remembering birthdays/anniversaries
4) Money
5) Their religious faith
6) Sexy lingerie

P3: THEY ALWAYS CARRY

1) Condoms
2) A first aid kit
3) A lucky charm
4) A length of rope
5) An old photograph
6) A pair of handcuffs

P4: THEY LIKE TO WEAR

1) Leather
2) Latex
3) All black
4) As little as possible
5) Boots
6) Something comfortable

P5: THEY ARE SEEKING

1) As many new partners as possible
2) To develop expertise
3) Justice
4) Acceptance
5) A challenge
6) A long-lost lover

P6: THE LESSON THEY NEED TO LEARN

1) To look before they leap
2) To be more open-minded
3) Responsibility
4) Patience
5) To let go of bitterness
6) To relax

CHARACTERS FOR BDSM FICTION

It's more important, for a BDSM-themed story, to have some or all of your main characters aware of their own kinks – if no one knows what they are doing, the story will take too long to get off the ground.

Roll once to establish gender/orientation.
1) Dominant female
2) Dominant male
3) Genderqueer/genderfluid dominant
4) Submissive male
5) Submissive female
6) Genderqueer/genderfluid submissive

Roll again: Odd number means this character is a switch.

Or, if you prefer, just pick a set of four charts, roll for the aspects and then decide for yourself what gender/sex/identity/orientation would suit the person who has appeared in your mind.

Now you will roll four times to establish four specific aspects to this character.

DOMINANT FEMALE

A: HER DAY JOB

1) Retail work
2) Lawyer
3) Care worker
4) Police officer
5) Jeweller
6) Model

B: A NOTICEABLE FACT ABOUT HER APPEARANCE

1) She is a BBW (Big Beautiful Woman)
2) She has dyed hair
3) She is petite
4) She has a tattoo
5) She has one or more scars
6) She is small-breasted

C: THE KINKY THING SHE LIKES BEST

1) Restraint
2) Impact play
3) Orgasm control
4) Hoods and masks
5) Mindfuckery
6) Domestic/personal service

D: THE MAIN THING MOTIVATING HER ACTIONS IS

1) To crush a rival
2) To explore dominance
3) To get over her ex
4) To find the perfect partner
5) To overcome a personal weakness
6) The pursuit of pleasure

DOMINANT MALE

A: AN ASPECT OF HIS APPEARANCE

1) He is bearded
2) He is short
3) He has a facial piercing
4) He has long hair
5) He wears glasses
6) He has a lot of body hair

B: THE MAIN THING MOTIVATING HIS ACTIONS IS

1) To find his soulmate
2) To improve his confidence
3) To get his revenge
4) Self-discovery
5) The pursuit of pleasure
6) To experience something new

C: HIS DAY JOB

1) Teacher
2) Florist
3) Designer
4) Estate agent
5) Medic
6) Waiter

D: HIS FAVOURITE KINK IS

1) Rope
2) Forced orgasms
3) Impact play
4) Oral service
5) Masks and hoods
6) Forced nudity

GENDERQUEER/GENDERFLUID DOMINANT

A: FAVOURITE KINK

1) High protocol
2) Spanking
3) Group sex
4) Rope
5) Edge play
6) Orgasm control

B: DAY JOB

1) IT consultant
2) Dancer
3) Gardener
4) Manager
5) Driver
6) Cleaner

C: AN ASPECT OF PHYSICAL APPEARANE

1) Hair dyed rainbow colours
2) Full lips
3) Fashionable
4) Very thin
5) Wears a lot of make up
6) Tall

D: MAIN MOTIVATION

1) To gain confidence
2) To move on after a breakup
3) The pursuit of pleasure
4) To become famous
5) To have fun and avoid commitment
6) To make money

FEMALE SUBMISSIVE

A: MAIN MOTIVATION

1) To satisfy her curiosity
2) To prove a point
3) The pursuit of pleasure
4) Revenge
5) Self-discovery
6) To make a good impression

B: FAVOURITE KINK

1) Fucking
2) Rope
3) Spanking
4) Enforced nudity
5) Roleplay
6) Being blindfolded

C: AN ASPECT OF HER PHYSICAL APPEARANCE

1) Short hair
2) Long legs
3) Terrible dress sense
4) Lots of piercings
5) Beautiful hands
6) Crooked teeth

D: DAY JOB

1) Pilot
2) Works in catering
3) Dentist
4) Head of HR
5) Taxi driver
6) MP

MALE SUBMISSIVE

A: DAY JOB

1) Barrister
2) Park keeper
3) Sells advertising space
4) Chef
5) Jeweller
6) Ticket inspector

B: AN ASPECT OF HIS PHYSICAL APPEARANCE

1) Long hair
2) Very skinny
3) Walks with a slight limp
4) Has facial hair
5) Has big feet
6) Is quite nondescript looking

C: MAIN MOTIVATION

1) To recover from a breakup
2) To improve his status
3) Self-discovery
4) To overcome fear
5) To have fun
6) To have a lot more orgasms

D: HIS FAVOURITE KINK

1) Pegging
2) Humiliation
3) Bondage
4) Impact play
5) Chastity
6) Wet and messy play

GENDERQUEER/GENDERFLUID SUBMISSIVE

A: AN ASPECT OF THEIR PHYSICAL APPEARANCE

1) An extreme hairstyle
2) Wears glasses
3) Favours bright colours
4) Has a birthmark/beauty spot on the face
5) Is very thin
6) Has an intimate piercing

B: MAIN MOTIVATION

1) To create great fetish art
2) To find a soulmate
3) To outwit an enemy
4) To discover a new kink
5) To be taken seriously
6) The pursuit of pleasure

C: FAVOURITE KINK

1) Caning
2) Edge play
3) Blindfolds
4) Restraint
5) Exhibitionism
6) Buttplugs

D: DAY JOB

1) Hairdresser
2) IT support
3) Minicab driver
4) Vet
5) Solicitor
6) Shelf stacker

STORY STARTERS

These charts are in sets of four, so you will roll once for each chart. This gives you four building blocks to base a story on. If you're not happy with the options given, roll again: getting an odd number means you can choose one result to discard; an even number means you can choose one item to roll again for a different option.

These charts are mainly for generating a short story, so the baseline assumption is there will be two main characters: a protagonist and the person with whom the protagonist will have sex. Unless specified, the gender/gender identity/orientation of your characters is up to you, and the charts are mostly open to quite a lot of interpretation.

If you are using this book in a writer's group, you can add an extra chart made up of suggestions from group members – or you can make up an additional chart if you are working alone, if you like.

SET 1

A: WHO IS YOUR PROTAGONIST?

1) An artist
2) Recently divorced
3) A teacher or educator of some kind
4) A criminal
5) A celebrity
6) A bit of rough

B: WHERE DOES THE MAIN ACTION TAKE PLACE?

1) On a cruise ship
2) On a farm
3) In a hotel
4) At a station
5) On a beach
6) In the workplace

C: AN OBJECT WHICH PLAYS AN IMPORTANT PART IN THE STORY

1) A bag
2) A pair of handcuffs
3) A bottle of wine
4) A camera
5) A book
6) A sex toy

D: A KEY CHARACTERISTIC OF THE PERSON YOUR PROTAGONIST ENCOUNTERS

1) The person is heartbroken
2) The person is shy
3) The person is not interested in kink
4) The person is very spiritual
5) The person is sports-mad
6) The person is arrogant.

(Writers' group additional chart: six different options to add another character)

SET 2

A YOUR PROTAGONIST IS/IDENTIFIES AS

1) Lesbian
2) Gay
3) Bisexual
4) Trans
5) Queer
6) Straight

B THIS UNEXPECTED EVENT TAKES PLACE EARLY ON

1) There is a storm
2) There is a road accident
3) Someone is arrested
4) The ex-partner of either the protagonist or the person the protagonist is attracted to appears
5) Something which appears to be paranormal activity occurs
6) Someone makes a proposal

C YOUR PROTAGONIST'S EMOTIONAL STATE AT THE BEGINNING OF THE STORY

1) Vengeful
2) Horny
3) Calm
4) Happy
5) Scared
6) Loving

D AN ASPECT OF YOUR PROTAGONIST'S PHYSICAL APPEARANCE

1) Protagonist has grey hair
2) Protagonist is toned and muscly
3) Protagonist has a limb in a plaster cast
4) Protagonist is barefoot
5) Protagonist is very short
6) Protagonist is wearing fancy dress

(Writers' group additional chart: six possible locations for your story)

SET 3

A: THE TIME THE MAIN EVENT HAPPENS

1) Early morning
2) Lunchtime
3) In summer
4) More than 10 years ago
5) Midnight
6) At Hallowe'en

B: AN OBJECT WHICH PLAYS AN IMPORTANT PART IN THE STORY

1) A whip
2) A corset
3) A four-poster bed
4) A cucumber
5) A latex hood or mask
6) An aphrodisiac

C: YOUR PROTAGONIST IS

1) Bisexual
2) Submissive
3) Inexperienced
4) Dominant
5) Has a bad reputation
6) Gorgeous

D: THE OTHER MAIN CHARACTER

1) Is timid
2) Is famous
3) Has a disability
4) Is a switch
5) Is deeply religious
6) Is over-confident

(Writers' group additional chart: six different aspects of a character's physical appearance)

SET 4

A: AT THE BEGINNING OF THE STORY,
YOUR PROTAGONIST...

1) Is hiding something
2) Is regretting something
3) Is angry about something
4) Is celebrating something
5) Is looking for something
6) Is afraid of something

B: THE TYPE OF SEX YOUR PROTAGONIST
LIKES THE BEST

1) Oral
2) Anal
3) Kinky
4) Romantic and loving
5) A new experience
6) Your protagonist is only attracted to people with a particular body type

C: THE SETTING/BACKGROUND/CONTEXT OF YOUR STORY

1) There are extreme weather conditions
2) Civil war or rioting is going on
3) There's a festival
4) It's an ordinary working day
5) It's a formal occasion
6) It's your protagonist's birthday

D: ONE OF YOUR MAIN CHARACTERS IS WEARING

1) High heels
2) Rubber
3) A hat
4) Handcuffs
5) Inappropriate clothing
6) Nipple clamps

(Writers' group additional chart: six different unexpected events that might happen)

SET 5

A: AN ASPECT OF YOUR PROTAGONIST'S PHYSICAL APPEARANCE

1) The protagonist is tattooed
2) The protagonist wears glasses
3) The protagonist has one or more piercings
4) The protagonist is large
5) The protagonist wears too much make up
6) The protagonist is wearing a mask

B: YOUR PROTAGONIST WANTS SOMETHING

1) Status
2) Adventure
3) To be tied up
4) To get together with the person the protagonist has a crush on
5) To defeat a rival
6) Sex

C: AS THE STORY OPENS...

1) Someone's crying
2) Someone's dancing
3) Someone's lost
4) Someone's worried
5) Someone's lying
6) Someone's surprised

D: THE MAIN EROTIC ELEMENT OF THE STORY INVOLVES

1) Nudity
2) A threesome
3) A spanking
4) A blindfold
5) Orgasm denial
6) Masturbation

(Writers' group additional chart: six different objects that might feature)

SET 6

A: WHEN DOES THE STORY TAKE PLACE?

1) Sunday afternoon
2) Saturday night
3) Monday morning
4) The protagonist's birthday
5) Midweek, 9-5
6) New Year's Day

B: YOUR PROTAGONIST...

1) Is lonely
2) Dresses very well
3) Is bisexual
4) Has a secret
5) Is a good dancer
6) Is bald

C: YOUR OTHER MAIN CHARACTER...

1) Is visually impaired
2) Is very promiscuous
3) Has dyed hair
4) Has low self-esteem
5) Is extremely superstitious
6) Has a facial piercing

D: THE MAIN SEXUAL INTERACTION TAKES PLACE...

1) Outside
2) At work
3) On a plane
4) In a cave
5) Over the phone
6) After a row

(Writers' group additional chart: six different options for a sexy outfit someone wears)

SET 7

A: WHEN THE STORY BEGINS, YOUR PROTAGONIST WANTS

1) Fame
2) An open relationship
3) A willing slave
4) To experiment with BDSM
5) To win back an ex-lover
6) A proposal

B: AT FIRST SIGHT, YOUR PROTAGONIST'S LOVE OBJECT APPEARS

1) Intimidating
2) Very attractive
3) Unhappy
4) Wealthy
5) Hostile
6) An expert

C: THE MAJOR PLOT EVENT IS...

1) An explosion
2) A lost key
3) Someone running away
4) Something important is forgotten
5) Someone gets very drunk
6) Prolonged sexual frustration

D: AT SOME POINT, THESE WORDS ARE SPOKEN

1) You're so beautiful
2) Can you help me?
3) What was that?
4) It's too much
5) I'm coming
6) Kiss me

(Writers' group additional chart: six different physical attributes for the love object)

SET 8

A: THE STORY CENTRES ON

1) A refusal
2) A fright
3) An argument
4) A visit to a sex shop
5) A love triangle
6) An unusual job offer

B: THE PERSON THE PROTAGONIST DESIRES

1) Is new in town
2) Has recently made a dramatic change to their appearance
3) Is from a very different ethnic, cultural and/or economic background to the protagonist
4) Charms absolutely everyone
5) Is the subject of worrying rumours
6) Appears unavailable

C: A CHARACTER TRAIT OF THE PROTAGONIST

1) Loves food
2) Is a good dancer
3) Enjoys making sex toys or fetish equipment
4) Believes in the supernatural
5) Was mistreated by a previous partner
6) Is extravagant

D: THE STORY MAINLY TAKES PLACE

1) At a party
2) During a conference or convention
3) In the countryside
4) In the city centre
5) In the middle of nowhere
6) Early in the morning

(Writers' group additional chart: six different kinds of sex or kink toy that might be used)

SET 9

A: AN IMPORTANT OBJECT IN THE STORY

1) A collar
2) A vibrator
3) A key
4) A pair of shoes
5) A mask
6) A phone

B: THE PROTAGONIST WANTS

1) To follow a dream
2) To learn more about a particular kink activity
3) To get over an ex partner
4) A particular sex scenario with a specific person
5) To overcome a weakness
6) To be adored

C: A KEY ASPECT OF THE OTHER MAIN CHARACTER'S APPEARANCE

1) The person wears revealing clothes
2) The person has very short hair
3) The person has a scar
4) The person wears a lot of jewellery
5) The person is big
6) The person is scruffy

D: THE EVENTS OF THE STORY TAKE PLACE

1) Within 24 hours
2) Within a week
3) Within a month
4) Within a season
5) Within a weekend
6) Within a year

(Writers' group additional chart: six different locations for sex to take place)

SET 10

A: YOUR PROTAGONIST'S WORST FAULT

1) Laziness
2) Arrogance
3) Jealousy
4) A quick temper
5) Carelessness
6) Selfishness

B: A LOCATION FOR THE MAIN EVENT

1) A photo studio
2) A field
3) The seaside
4) A play party
5) A hotel bedroom
6) A station

C: YOUR PROTAGONIST'S KINKY STYLE

1) Spanking and CP
2) Sensual or spiritual
3) Rough and primal
4) Switchy and playful
5) Likes humiliation and degradation
6) High protocol D/s

D: AN ASPECT OF YOUR PROTAGONIST'S APPEARANCE

1) Has a kink-related tattoo
2) Has long fingernails
3) Is toned and athletic-looking
4) Has a shaved head
5) Is very pale
6) Has an intimate piercing

(Writers' group additional chart: six different surprising things the love object says)

REBOOT, RETHINK, REVITALISE

Sometimes a story just gets stuck, and you have no idea how to proceed. Either there are too many obstacles in the way, or too few. Maybe the character who seemed so enticing has started to get on your nerves. Still, somewhere in what looks like a big mess, there might be a salvageable story. Here are a few tricks you could try...

ONE BIG CHANGE

Roll once and see what you get.

1) Remove a major character
2) Introduce a new major character
3) Change the viewpoint (e.g. from first person to deep third)
4) Change the setting (from rural to urban or vice versa)
5) Change the era (from past to present or vice versa)
6) Change the protagonist: let a different character be the focus of the story

CHALLENGE YOUR CHARACTERS

1) Change the protagonist's orientation
2) Flip the gender/gender identity of those in the main relationship
3) Flip the protagonist's erotic experience level (from novice to expert or vice versa)
4) Give the protagonist a very specific and relatively niche fetish
5) Change the socioeconomic background of one or the other of your main couple
6) Change the protagonist's physical abilities or health

MAKE SOMETHING HAPPEN

If the plot is going absolutely nowhere, try introducing danger, conflict or at least misunderstanding. If you're not too far into the story, you can just throw something into the mix, though some of these potential events might need a little bit of foreshadowing in the earlier chapters...

Choose either Chart Set A or Chart Set B.

Roll once for the first chart, then again for the chart matching what you got the first time.

CHART SET A

1) A natural phenomenon
2) An accident
3) An unexpected person appears
4) Bad news
5) Good news
6) Possible paranormal activity

A: NATURAL PHENOMENON

1) Earthquake
2) Flood
3) Lightning strikes
4) Hailstorm
5) Unseasonable heat
6) Fog

B: ACCIDENT

1) Someone has a fall
2) Car crash
3) Something gets broken
4) An animal is involved
5) A joke goes wrong
6) A train derails

C: UNEXPECTED PERSON

1) A police officer
2) An ex-partner
3) A long-lost relative
4) A burglar
5) A celebrity
6) Someone selling something

D: BAD NEWS

1) Job loss
2) A relative has been hurt in an accident
3) Protagonist is diagnosed with a serious illness
4) A plan collapses
5) Pregnancy
6) There is imminent danger

E: GOOD NEWS

1) A truth is discovered
2) Unexpected financial windfall
3) A danger has been averted
4) Pregnancy
5) A good job is on offer
6) A contest has been won

F: POSSIBLE PARANORMAL ACTIVITY

1) Possible UFO sighting
2) A visit to a spooky location
3) Poltergeist activity
4) Someone displays psychic powers
5) A dream comes true
6) Possible ghost sighting

CHART SET B

1) The love object disappears
2) A crime is committed
3) An unexpected person arrives
4) A mistake is made
5) Someone gets a phone call
6) A news story breaks

A: LOVE OBJECT DISAPPEARS

1) The person has been arrested
2) The person has lost phone/money/both and is stranded
3) The person has been taken ill
4) A close friend is in trouble and needs immediate help
5) The person got stuck on public transport
6) There has been a misunderstanding

B: A CRIME IS COMMITTED

1) Something is stolen
2) Threats have been made
3) Someone's car is vandalised
4) A fire is started
5) Fraud
6) Someone gets attacked

C: AN UNEXPECTED PERSON

1) An attractive rival
2) A long-lost relative
3) A private detective
4) Someone who was believed dead
5) A journalist chasing a story
6) An angry employer

D: A MISTAKE IS MADE

1) Someone's bank account is frozen
2) Someone got the wrong date for a major event
3) Someone jumped to the wrong conclusion
4) Someone got on the wrong train
5) The wrong bag was picked up and taken away
6) A laptop was left open with no password protection

E: AN UNEXPECTED PHONE CALL

1) It's the wrong number
2) It's threatening
3) It's from the ex who broke the protagonist's heart
4) It's the police
5) The recipient of the call refuses to say who it was
6) A close friend is in serious trouble

F: A NEWS STORY BREAKS

1) Someone has 'sold their story'
2) The head of state has died
3) There is going to be a change to the law regarding sex
4) War is imminent or has just broken out
5) Extreme weather warning
6) One or more very dangerous individuals have escaped from prison

THEMES

Sometimes it's fun to take a specific concept or setting and see what happens if you mess it up a bit. There are a few sub-genres in popular fiction (the Christmas feelgood romance, the wedding saga) that might seem so overused that they are not worth bothering about. But, if you add in a few random factors, you never know where your imagination might take you. Here are a few possibilities to play with.

These charts are probably best suited to novellas or novels, and especially those that are more at the erotic romance end of the scale, where you have enough room to put a little more plot in.

THEME A: SEASONS AND SPECIAL DAYS

Roll once for the time of year your story will take place.

1) January/February
2) March/April
3) May/June
4) July/August
5) September/October
6) November/December

There are various annual holidays, official celebrations, special days and seasonal rituals, obviously, with some being better known than others. If you can't think of anything that inspires you, or the only holiday that falls around the time of year you got in the first roll is not at all sexy, then you could invent a local pageant, historical commemoration, fair or show for your characters to deal with.

Roll again for your protagonist's attitude towards the 'big day/week'.

- **Odds** – the protagonist loves to celebrate and participate
- **Evens** – the protagonist hates the event, or tries to avoid it.

Roll again for the weather conditions.

- **Odds** – the weather is perfectly appropriate to the time of year
- **Evens** – the weather is unseasonal and may spoil the event

And roll once for each of the following charts.

A: PROTAGONIST'S KEY ISSUE

1) Is far from home
2) Is remembering a previous year when this holiday/event was taking place
3) Needs to make a major life change
4) Recovering from illness or a serious injury
5) Is filled with regrets
6) Wants to make things perfect for someone else

B: THE POTENTIAL PARTNER FOR THE PROTAGONIST

1) Is a seasonal worker or part of event crew
2) A local official
3) An activist
4) An artist
5) A tourist
6) A shopkeeper or local trader

C: THE PROTAGONIST OFTEN WEARS

1) A hat
2) Bright colours
3) Uncomfortable footwear
4) A significant piece of jewellery
5) Signature scent
6) Gloves

D: WHEN THE PROTAGONIST FIRST MEETS THE POTENTIAL PARTNER

1) One mistakes the other for someone else
2) There is an immediate physical attraction
3) One is at a serious disadvantage
4) One of them is naked
5) A discussion about sex is taking place
6) The ex of one of them is present

THEME B: WEDDINGS AND COMMITMENTS

First roll:

- **Odds** – the ceremony goes wrong or doesn't happen
- **Evens** – the ceremony is satisfactorily completed.

Second roll:

- **Odds** – the ceremony is where the story begins
- **Evens** – the ceremony is the climax of the story

Then roll once each for the following four charts.

A: TYPE OF EVENT

1) Religious wedding
2) Civil partnership
3) Collaring ceremony
4) Handfasting
5) Wedding reception
6) Secular wedding

B: YOUR PROTAGONIST IS

1) Bride/groom
2) Best man/chief bridesmaid/equivalent
3) Ex-partner of one of those about to be married
4) Celebrant, minister or registrar
5) Guest
6) Catering crew

C: THERE WILL BE SOME EROTIC INTERACTION

1) In a vehicle
2) In a kitchen
3) Outside
4) Somewhere there is a risk of being discovered by third parties
5) Very early in the morning
6) While a significant piece of music is playing

D: PROTAGONIST'S MAIN MOTIVATION

1) To be the object of desire
2) Erotic transcendence
3) Public validation
4) Payback
5) To come to the rescue
6) Ownership

THEME C: FESTIVALS AND CONVENTIONS

First roll:

The type of event is:
- **Odds** – small-scale and local
- **Evens** - Large, attracts an international audience

Second roll:

1) A rock festival
2) A BDSM convention
3) A horror fans' convention
4) A folk festival
5) A literary festival
6) An adult industry trade event

Now roll for each of the following four charts.

A: PROTAGONIST

1) Organiser
2) First time visitor
3) Performer/presenter
4) Groupie or superfan
5) Frequent attendee
6) Crew member

B: CONFLICT

1) Star performer cancels at the last minute
2) Local opposition to the event
3) Protagonist battling heartbreak
4) Rivalry between performers/presenters
5) Someone decides to come out
6) Sexual dissatisfaction

C: AN OBJECT WHICH IS SIGNIFICANT TO THE STORY

1) A faulty microphone
2) A whip
3) A nude photograph
4) A ring
5) A bottle of lube
6) A musical instrument

D: THE PERSON THE PROTAGONIST DESIRES

1) Is a celebrity
2) Has a reputation for leading others astray
3) Is ordinary-looking apart from one striking feature
4) Doesn't want to be there
5) Has several admirers
6) Is hiding something

THEME D: WORKING RELATIONSHIPS

First roll: what kind of work environment is your story set in?

1) Catering/hospitality
2) Sport/exercise/fitness
3) The adult industry
4) Medicine
5) Outdoors
6) Media/the arts

Second roll:

- **Odds** – High-earning, glamorous end of the industry
- **Evens** – small-scale, local, struggling

Now roll for each of the following four charts.

A: OBSTACLES IN THE WAY OF THE CENTRAL RELATIONSHIP

1) The characters work for rival companies
2) One is considerably senior to the other
3) One is trying to get the other's business closed down
4) One appears to have stolen the other's ideas
5) The company is struggling and may go under
6) One is making a comeback after a spectacular fuckup

B: PROTAGONIST'S ATTITUDE TOWARDS SEX/RELATIONSHIPS

1) Workaholic, no time for a relationship
2) Has a variety of partners and is open about the fact
3) Has a secret fetish
4) Has been hurt in the past and is reluctant to date again
5) Inexperienced but eager
6) Used to being desired by almost everyone

C: THE CHARACTERS FIRST HAVE SEX

1) On a business trip
2) When they are trapped somewhere together
3) After one comforts the other following a setback or distressing incident
4) At an industry party/award ceremony
5) When they encounter one another unexpectedly
6) Before the story starts

D: PROTAGONIST IS INITIALLY ATTRACTED BY THE OTHER MAIN CHARACTER BECAUSE OF

1) Beautiful eyes
2) Formal clothing
3) A discreet indication that the other is kinky
4) Revelation of an unexpected skill
5) Sexy voice
6) An act of kindness

THEME E: TRAVELLING

First roll: why is your protagonist away from home?

- **Odds** - Business
- **Evens** - Pleasure

Second roll: protagonist's travel circumstances

1) Travelling alone
2) Travelling with a large group
3) Travelling with a small group
4) Travelling in a positive frame of mind
5) Would rather be at home
6) Travelling under false pretences

Then roll once each for the following four charts.

A: YOUR PROTAGONIST'S ACCOMMODATION

1) Luxury hotel
2) Camping
3) Staying with a friend who lives in the area
4) Budget hotel
5) On a boat
6) Protagonist will sort something out on arrival

B: THE LOVE OBJECT

1) A fellow traveller
2) A local resident
3) An ex-partner who unexpectedly reappears
4) A visiting celebrity
5) A mysterious stranger
6) Hotelier, chef, tour guide or similar

C: THE TYPE OF LOCATION

1) Big city
2) Beach resort
3) Long haul destination (for the protagonist)
4) Mountain district
5) Somewhere remote and isolated
6) Somewhere with a great deal of history

D THE SEX FACTOR

1) Protagonist has not had sex for a long time
2) Protagonist or love object is mildly kinky
3) Protagonist is romantic and gentle
4) Love object is inexperienced
5) Love object is bitter and jaded
6) Protagonist is seeking something naughty and spontaneous

WORKED EXAMPLES

By way of a quick demonstration, here are a few samples of character creation and how constructing one or two characters can get you up and running with a potential story. There is also a rough outline of a short erotic story. The charts used and the combinations rolled are set out below.

TWO CHARACTERS AND A CONCEPT

CHARACTER 1

From chart V4 Dresses smartly
From chart M1: Has traditional values
From chart P5: Wants as many new partners as possible.

So, already, I've got a character with a potential internal conflict – how to balance traditional values with a desire for lots of new sexual partners?

Milly is in her early 40s and has always lived in a small, quiet town. She was brought up to take a lot of pride in her appearance, to work hard and put other people before herself. She married quite young, but had no children. However, after 15 years, she threw out her husband, who had been repeatedly unfaithful. She decided that being good hadn't done her any favours, and so she would throw herself into having all the fun she missed out on when she was younger. She discovered erotic fiction and, shortly after that, online dating.

CHARACTER 2

From chart V1: Has beautiful hands
From chart M5: Is a daydreamer
From chart P2: Cares about sexy lingerie

Bette runs a shop specialising in beautiful lingerie, much of which she makes and designs herself. She likes making women look wonderful and helping them to feel good about themselves. She's recently started stocking a range of sex toys that are visually appealing as well as reasonably priced, and sometimes imagines herself becoming famous as someone who changes women's sex lives for the better.

The 'beautiful hands' aspect didn't come in straight away as I started thinking about someone working with their hands, designing and crafting. But I held the option, because there was still the possibility of those hands being the first thing that draw in a potential romantic or sexual partner.

Having got that far, I've already got the bones of a story – Milly walks into Bette's shop one day, and there is an instant attraction between them, but Milly's not quite ready to admit she likes women as well as men, and she certainly doesn't want to tie herself down with another relationship just yet...

CREATING A CHARACTER FOR BDSM FICTION

I rolled once to establish gender and BDSM orientation and got Dominant Male.

The next four rolls established that this Dom:
- Has a lot of body hair
- Is looking to experience something new
- Works by day in a florist's shop
- His favourite kink is rope.

Simon might look like a cuddly teddy bear, but he has a deliciously twisted mean streak in his character. He is popular on the local shibari scene, but is beginning to realise he wants something more: to explore the formal type of D/s.

I decided at this point that the floristry wasn't particularly relevant to the picture I was beginning to build of Simon, so left it out.

Simon becomes involved with Jojo, a genderqueer switch, and they begin to build a relationship that doesn't quite go as expected. A key scene is when Jojo gives Simon a full body shave but this is a personal service thing, not Jojo topping Simon... However, it begins to look more and more likely that Simon will allow Jojo to tie him and perhaps even suspend him.

STORY STARTERS

From Chart 3:

- Time the main event happens: Midnight
- Object which plays an important part in the story: Aphrodisiac
- Your protagonist is: Dominant
- Your other main character is: Over-confident

I came up with the following outline for a short story, possibly flash fiction:

A play party is taking place in a large house. Mistress Dani and her friends have been chatting about the latest fetish scene gossip, and particularly about Greg, a young man who is new to BDSM and a bit too full of himself. He seems generally inclined to go out of his way to be rude to Dani, and her friends have recently been teasing her that it's because he's attracted to her. Dani tells them he has always identified himself as a top, so she rather doubts this. Though she doesn't say this to anyone, she finds Greg attractive, as well, and suspects he has a submissive streak he is trying to conceal.

Midway through the evening, there is a conversation about aphrodisiacs, and whether they work or not. Someone is joking about the bowl of punch at the table and its 'secret ingredient'. The party hosts join in on the joke, making references to an 'old family recipe' and the other exciting and surprising things that have happened when they have served punch at parties. Much of this conversation is clearly for the benefit of Greg and the handful of other guests who have never been to a party at this house before.

At midnight, a toast is drunk, or the punchbowl is refilled: Greg drinks some punch and, shortly after that, he approaches Dani and asks her if she will top him. He enjoys the experience and so does she, and they both wonder, later on, if there was anything in all that 'nonsense' about an aphrodisiac in the punchbowl.

The results I got did not actually specify that the dominant protagonist had to be female, nor did the over-confident character have to be male: I have a general tendency to write femdom when I write kinky erotica. But the scenario outlined above would probably work just as well if it were male dom and submissive woman, or M/M or F/F, or with genderqueer characters.

ADDITIONAL CHARTS

CHART: _____

1	
2	
3	
4	
5	
6	

CHART: _

1	
2	
3	
4	
5	
6	

CHART: _____

1	
2	
3	
4	
5	
6	

CHART: _____

1	
2	
3	
4	
5	
6	

CHART: _

1	
2	
3	
4	
5	
6	

CHART: _

1	
2	
3	
4	
5	
6	

CHART: _

1	
2	
3	
4	
5	
6	

SELECTED BOOKS BY ZAK JANE KEIR

GOODBYE MODERATION: GLUTTONY

Find out more: books2read.com/gluttony

RULE 34

Find out more: books2read.com/rule34

SILVER DESIRE

Find out more: books2read.com/silverdesire

STICKY FINGERS & WARM LEATHERETTE

Find out more: books2read.com/sticky-fingers

BLACK HEART

Find out more: books2read.com/black-heart

Printed in Great Britain
by Amazon

83067000R00061